CONCORDANCE

Mei-mei Berssenbrugge

poetry

Kiki Smith

art

Kelsey Street Press

Publication of this book was made possible by generous donations from
the LEF Foundation, Cris Arguedas, Rena Bransten, Tecoah Bruce,
Sharon Gillin, Howard Hertz, Jane Lurie, Anthony and Celeste Meier,
Diane Middlebrook, Roselyne Swig, Eileen Tabios, Earlene and
John Taylor, and Martha and Peter Wilson.

Series produced by Rena Rosenwasser.
Special thanks to Robert Rosenwasser for his assistance in design.

Acknowledgements:
"Concordance", Part #1 was published in *The American Poet*.
"Red Quiet", Part #2 was published in *Bomb*.
Concordance was published by the
Rutgers Center for Innovative Print and Paper.

Library of Congress Cataloging-in-Publication Data

Berssenbrugge, Mei-mei, 1947–
  Concordance / Mei-mei Berssenbrugge, poetry; Kiki Smith, art.—1st ed.
    p. cm.
  ISBN-13: 978-0-932716-67-5 (alk. paper)
  I. Smith, Kiki, 1954– II. Title.
  PS3552.E77C66 2006
  811'.54—dc22

     2006004176

Kelsey Street Press   kelseyst.com

All orders to Small Press Distribution
510.524.1668
800.869.7553

orders@spdbooks.org

for the frogs and toads

CONCORDANCE

1.

Writing encounters one who
does not write and I don't try
for him, but face-to-face draw
you onto a line or flight like a
break that may be extended,
the way milkweed filling space
above the field is 'like' reading.

Then it's possible to undo
misunderstanding from inside
by tracing the flight or thread of
empty space running through
things, even a relation that's
concordant.

Seeds disperse in summer air.

Sunrays cease to represent parallel
passages in a book, i.e., not coming
from what I see and feel.

Relation is in the middle, relay,
flower description *to* flower
becoming of the eye between light
and heart.

Now, information has released
imaginative function from authors.

I send the interrupted line over the
top of space, past the middle
cinematically, when you no longer
stand what you put up with before.

At night, part of her numbed to
pain and part woke to what occurred.

Working backward in sleep, the last thing you numbed to is what wakes you.

What if that image were Eros as words?

I write to you and you feel me.

What would it be like if you contemplated my words and I felt you?

Animals, an owl, frog, open their eyes, and a mirror forms on the ground.

When insight comes in a dream,
and events the next day
illuminate it, this begins your
streaming consciousness,
synchronicity, asymptotic lines
of the flights of concordances.

An owl opens its eyes in deep
woods.

For the first time, I write and you
don't know me.

Milkweed I touch floats.

2.

One experiences another's energy
as stress.

At first, I felt attacked by this
attribution of the symptoms of my
illnesses.

I was frightened thoughts and
feelings could be externalized.

Then, I saw sunrise frequencies
emanate from your body, like music.

An excited person in light absorbs
wavelengths she herself gives off, as
if light were the nutrient for feeling.

Color is a mirror where we see
ourselves with living things, scarlet
neck feathers, infant asleep across
your heart, like-to-like.

Attention gives light: shine on a
baby's calf; as he hears what I say,
I become that.

Look at my body as light
reflecting the thought and feeling:
it's not safe here.

Remove anxiousness over persons
you yearn for, stepping back to
observe, like an animal in the fourth
dimension.

Since animals don't judge, their
evolving cosmic skills are a source
of richness for us.

A bird lands on the rim of your tub;
a wolf licks your baby's head.

When she cries and the part of
you who cries wakes, do you hold
her to suppress feeling?

Yearning can't be split and the animal
lost, ahead of time.

3.

My words unroll a plane of
consistence they do not pre-exist—
particles, fluxes the colors of spring.

Desire individuates through affects
and powers I place on a page or plane
of light vibrations, like a flowering
field.

His autonomic response is to
constrict breath against the feminine,
magnetism of gems, consciousness
emanating from stars symbiotic
with individuation.

When I hear ants are telepathic,
I see tiny words trying to
communicate.

Then, they file across my clock;
it's time to go.

Life manifests everywhere in the cosmos, but as we eliminate species here, we lose access to other realms.

So, discovering a new species is a great event.

Numinousness in the psyche emerges as from morphic fields, our wish for the animal tuning to its light or waveform, like the light of sex.

When you doubt this, you place
a piece of "someone" on a pedestal
to examine, a gap.

Breathe the shard back into yourself.

In your memory, scarlet feathers of a
beloved macaw begin a glow arising
from the exact color of connection.

Warmth, which was parallel, moves
across the shard, smoothes and makes
it porous, matter breath, light
materializing dear ants and dear words.

RED QUIET

1.

I look into his eyes and feel my
awareness expand to contain what he
will tell me, as if what he says is a
photograph of landscape and in my
mind will be a painting of "Hill,"
"Part of the Cliffs," "Purple Hills."

These words are the opposite of
verisimilitude.

Between his location and mine is
white space constituting the flow of
emotion on which we travel, when
moving awareness from a place
to a moment.

Ghost particles exist on the border between something that happens and increasing probability it will happen again.

Words spoken with force gather particles.

A person enters, and now my room is encased in dread.

Even so, I was too concerned, like a young girl trying to understand feelings through my feeling.

If existence is vibration, everything
creates sound — trees, heart cells.

Listeners, like water, resonate dread
in a blue vase, in glasses.

I send out an emotion of warmth,
welcome, the way scientists erase
sound with sound.

2.

When a person enters, space is
fragmented.

A red amaryllis in sun quarters the
breakfast room.

Each large petal extends a moment
vector into space, like the crystalline
structure of water freezing,
consciousness registering time.

The idea that red as in sex, love, will
open the gates of heaven is trying to
substitute a feeling of heaven for the
experience of heaven.

Red maintains a strong impression
of the body, while consciousness
flows along its inner images.

When an amaryllis bends toward
light and I don't turn it, I may still
change the feeling of it leaning in
my memory, whirling with the sun,
crossing from my experience to
larger probability.

My love for the blossom partakes of
transitions fields create with emotion.
I mean certain locations attract events.

So, I object to expending energy
trying to alleviate a situation with
horticulture.

I look into a blossom, and its image
sinks into me like winter rain.

A cause is not determined, when I
perceive, with its intense presence,
the isolation of the *red* hue, as in
white space previously mentioned.

3.

Our conversation is a wing below my
consciousness, like organization
in blowing cloth, eddies of water, its
order of light on film with no lens.

A higher resonance of story finds its
way to higher organization: data swirl
into group dreams.

Then story surfaces, as if recognized,
flies buzzing in your room suddenly
translate to "Oh! You're crying."

So, here I hug the old person, who's not "light" until I embrace him.

My happiness at seeing him, my French suit constitute at the interface of wing and occasion.

Postulate whether the friendship is truly fulfilling.

Reduce by small increments your worry about the nature of compassion or the chill of emotional identification among girlfriends, your wish to be held in the consciousness of another, like a person waiting for you to wake.

Postulate the wave nature of wanting
him to wait (white space) and the
quanta of fractal conflict, point to point,
along the outline of a petal, shore
from a small boat.

Words spoken with force create particles.

He calls the location of accidents a
morphic field; their recurrence is
resonance, as of an archetype with
the vibration of a seed.

*My last thoughts were bitter and
helpless*

Friends witnessing grief enter your
consciousness, illuminating your form,
so quiet comes.